The Twenty Children of Johann Sebastian Bach

BACH

JOHANN CHRISTOPH   ERNESTUS ANDREAS

CARL PHILIPP EMANUEL

JOHANN
CHRISTOPH

JOHANN
CHRISTIAN

ELISABETHA
JULIANE

CATHARINA
DOROTHEA

The
TWENTY
CHILDREN
of
Johann
Sebastian
Bach

BY DAVID ARKIN

✤

THE WARD RITCHIE PRESS

GOTTFRIED
HEINRICH

GOTTFRIED
BERNHARD

REGINE
SUSANNA

REGINE
JOHANNE

MARIA
SOPHIE

JOHANNE
CAROLINA

JOHANN
AUGUST

LEOPOLD
AUGUSTUS

WILHELM FRIEDEMANN

CHRISTIANE
SOPHIE

CHRISTIAN
GOTTLIEB

CHRISTIANE
DOROTHEA   CHRISTIANE
BENEDICTA

To my wife Beatrice

The author would like to thank
Jan and Kathy Aronoff, Joseph Simon,
Cas Duchow, and Dick and Mary Lewis
for their invaluable assistance
in preparing this book.

Copyright © 1968 by The Ward Ritchie Press
Library of Congress Catalog Card Number: 68-24458
Lithographed in the United States of America
By Anderson, Ritchie and Simon

The little family of Johann Sebastian Bach was trying bravely to keep itself going. Wilhelm Friedemann, eleven years old, was too young to be of very much help, and the other two boys were even younger. Carl Philipp Emanuel was only eight years old and Johann Gottfried Bernhard, seven.

And so Catharina Dorothea was trying to be very grown up for a thirteen-year-old, and was doing her best to care for a family that had lost a mother.

"I'm afraid I'm not taking care of the family as well as Mother used to," sighed Catharina Dorothea. "This is a job for a grown up person."

"You're doing very well," said her brother Wilhelm Friedemann, softly. And her father, the great musician Johann Sebastian, comforted her. "You are taking very good care of our family, Catharina."

But Johann Sebastian knew it was time to find someone who would help him care for his children. There was Anna Magdalena, and she loved him and his music very dearly. She was the daughter of Johann Caspar Wilcken, trumpeter at the court of the Duke of Weissenfels.

And so they were married in the Bach home in Cöthen, on December 3, 1721, with the children gathered around them.

The next week, Bach's patron, Prince Leopold of Anhalt-Cöthen, was also married. He had his own orchestra, and it played at the wedding.

Bach was concertmaster for Leopold's orchestra. He composed and performed chamber music and many concertos, overtures, and suites.

The young prince loved music very much and played on a number of instruments himself. He and Bach spent many glorious hours together over music. It was here, at Leopold's court, that Bach composed the great Brandenburg concertos.

The happiness of Bach and Prince Leopold was complete, and the music was a golden echo of that happiness.

But the new princess did not care for music. She did not like to see her husband spend so much time with the orchestra. And so the duke gave up his interest in music, and Bach decided it was time to leave Cöthen with his family.

The children were excited at leaving Cöthen.
They packed their belongings, their music and instruments.

To Leipzig, that great city of eastern Germany,
famous all over Europe for its fairs.

Farewells were said to the Prince and his bride,
and off they went on the long journey . . .

There Bach had gotten a position as Cantor and teacher of music
at St. Thomas' School, and there he would spend the rest of his life.

It was quite a task for the new family to get settled. And quite a task for a young bride of twenty. There was a family of six for Anna Magdalena to take care of. She found herself in the midst of

Cooking

and Sewing,

Marketing

and Cleaning.

In all the work, Catharina Dorothea was such a great help that
Anna Magdalena did not find it too great a burden. "You're like a kind
sister to me," she would say to Catharina. Even the boys helped, and
so did Johann Sebastian, although much of the time he was
busy at the school.

But most wonderful were the quiet hours at home, when he and
Anna Magdalena sang together at the clavichord—sang together the
glorious music of Johann Sebastian Bach, or played the clavier pieces he
had written in the little green book he had bound especially for her.

But things were not going too well at the new school. Many of Johann's students did not behave. They had poor voices. They did not love music, and they were rude and noisy in class.

The director of the school complained.

The musicians were underpaid and would not stay long at the job.

The organist of St. Thomas' School was so clumsy an accompanist that Bach once took off his wig and threw it at him!

The City Council was angry and scolded Bach.

Things got so bad that Bach wrote a letter applying for a job as musician at the court of the Emperor of Russia. Then events took another turn.

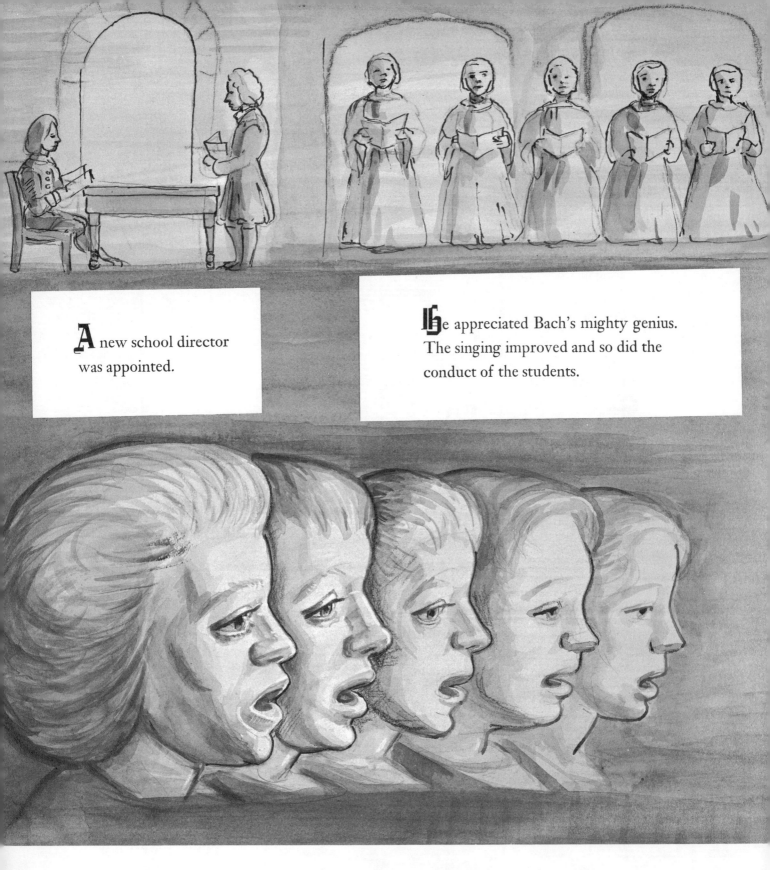

A new school director was appointed.

He appreciated Bach's mighty genius. The singing improved and so did the conduct of the students.

Bach's glorious music seemed to create a new harmony in the school, and it looked as if things would change for the better for Johann and his family. Perhaps they might be able to live and grow in Leipzig.

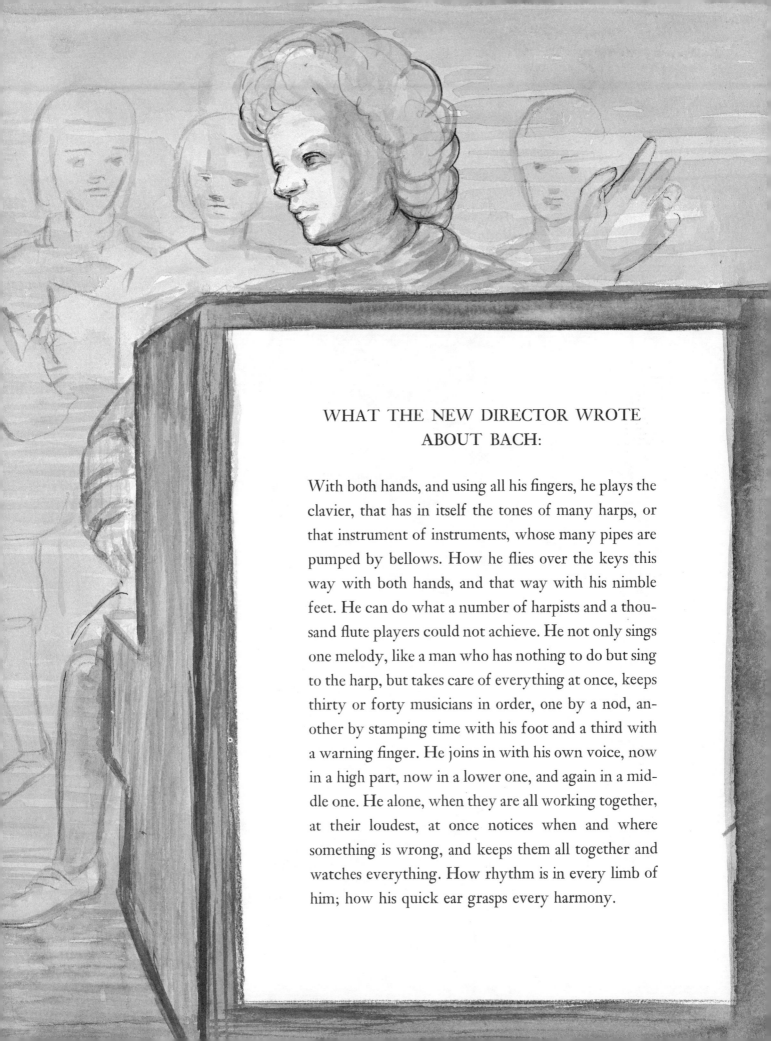

WHAT THE NEW DIRECTOR WROTE ABOUT BACH:

With both hands, and using all his fingers, he plays the clavier, that has in itself the tones of many harps, or that instrument of instruments, whose many pipes are pumped by bellows. How he flies over the keys this way with both hands, and that way with his nimble feet. He can do what a number of harpists and a thousand flute players could not achieve. He not only sings one melody, like a man who has nothing to do but sing to the harp, but takes care of everything at once, keeps thirty or forty musicians in order, one by a nod, another by stamping time with his foot and a third with a warning finger. He joins in with his own voice, now in a high part, now in a lower one, and again in a middle one. He alone, when they are all working together, at their loudest, at once notices when and where something is wrong, and keeps them all together and watches everything. How rhythm is in every limb of him; how his quick ear grasps every harmony.

And the family began to grow.

There were children,

and more children.

Some of Bach's best lullabys were composed
while walking the floor at night with
a baby in his arms.

But there was also sadness in the Bach family. Of the twenty children,
seven did not live.

But those who survived were wonderful children.
All of them could sing. And many could play a number of instruments.

And they assisted Papa Bach in St. Thomas' School and at the services in
St. Thomas' church. They helped pump the bellows of the organ,

They could write music,

and play the clavichord.

Or play the organ.

they wrote out the musical scores for the services and sang in the chorus when he presented his great musical work, "The Passion According to Saint Matthew."

Sometimes they would join the students of St. Thomas' School when they marched singing through the streets on holidays.

But Papa Bach did not approve of this because in cold weather
it was bad for their voices.

Johann Sebastian Bach gave great care to the musical education of his family. He prepared exercises for them to practice which have become great piano classics . . .

. . . classics like the "Little Clavier Book," the "Inventions," or the
immortal "Well-Tempered Clavichord" which he first prepared
for Wilhelm Friedemann.

From the rear windows of the Bach household in St. Thomas' School, they could look out on the Pleisse River, on the fields, the pleasant gardens, and the old mill.

Many a time, as the children played by the winding stream, they could
hear sounds coming from the great church—perhaps a rehearsal
for a cantata, or Papa Bach playing one of his great preludes.

ost wonderful of all were the times when the family gathered together at holidays with their friends. Then the immortal music of all the Bachs would ring out for the earth and heavens to hear.

Perhaps they would sing the Christmas Oratorio, or a cantata,
or maybe they would just make up music as they went along.

Bach's sons grew up to be much more famous than their father and were known all over Europe. Wilhelm Friedemann became organist at Dresden. He was called "the Dresden Bach."

And Carl Philipp Emanuel became known as master composer and virtuoso on the clavichord. He was at the court of King Frederick the Great of Prussia. He was called "the Berlin Bach."

Johann Christian Bach went to London, to follow Händel as the great musician at the court of King George III. He composed many operas and set a style which Mozart and Haydn followed. He was called "the London Bach."

And there was Johann Christoph Bach, also a celebrated composer.
Wherever there was music in Europe, there the name of Bach was heard.
And Christoph was called "the Bückeburg Bach."

Then there was Gottfried Heinrich, a great genius who remained a
child. He improvised deep, wild, sad songs. His music brought tears to
the eyes of his listeners. He always needed someone to take care of
him. ¶ Catharina Dorothea and her sisters, Regine Susanna and Johanne
Carolina, stayed with their mother and father.
They never married.

Elisabetha Juliane Friederica was courted by a merchant. She refused
him. "I can never marry anyone who is without music in his
heart," she told her father.

Later Elisabetha married Johann Christoph Altnikol, Bach's favorite pupil. Johann Sebastian composed a wedding cantata for the occasion.

Johann Sebastian Bach's greatest triumph came when Frederick the
Great, King of Prussia, asked Carl Philipp Emanuel to invite his father
to the palace. Frederick loved to play flute concertos with the royal

orchestra. The king asked Bach to improvise upon a tune that the king
made up. The music that came forth was glorious. The name of
Bach rang throughout the land.

In his later years, Bach was happy to stay quietly at home with Anna Magdalena and his remaining children, working steadily on his music.

The times were changing, and people wanted to hear lighter and gayer music. Italian opera became the rage, and Bach and his music were almost forgotten.

It was only after a hundred years that all mankind began to appreciate his sublime music and to realize that, of seven generations of wonderful musicians, he was the mightiest Bach of them all.

WORDS OF THIS BOOK

BACH: Bak—the 'k' is pronounced far back in the throat.

CANTOR: The conductor—the leader of a church singing group.

CHAMBER-MUSIC: Music played with a few instruments in a living room.

CHOIR: A group of singers in a church chorus.

CLAVICHORD: A musical instrument very much like a piano, made long ago.

CLAVIER: A clavichord.

IMPROVISE: To make up music as you go along.

JOHANN: Is pronounced yō-han.

OVERTURE: A piece played by an orchestra at the beginning of a musical dramatic work.

PATRON: A nobleman or king who hired musicians to play for him at the castle.

WELL-TEMPERED: A special way of tuning a clavichord.

THE 20 CHILDREN OF JOHANN SEBASTIAN BACH

Catharina Dorothea

Wilhelm Friedemann

Johann Christoph

Maria Sophie

Carl Philipp Emanuel

(Johann) Gottfried Bernhard

Leopold Augustus

Christiane Sophie (Henrietta)

Gottfried Heinrich

Christian Gottlieb

Elisabetha Juliane (Friederica)

Ernestus Andreas

Regine Johanne

Christiane Benedicta

Christiane Dorothea

Johann Christoph (Friedrich)

Johann August (Abraham)

Johann Christian

Johanne Carolina

Regine Susanna

The beginning of the first movement of the sixth Brandenburg Concerto in B flat major in full score.